EAS

JOKES

FOR KIDS

1. What is the Easter Bunny's favorite jewelry?

24 carrot gold.

2. What would happen if the Easter bunny met the rabbit of their dreams?

They would live hoppily ever after.

3.   What does the Easter Bunny do to stay in shape?

Egg-xercise.

4.   What kind of rabbit tells good jokes?

A funny bunny.

5.   Why would you not want to tell an Easter egg a good joke?

It may crack up.

6.   Where did the two rabbits go after their wedding?

On a bunnymoon.

7. **How would you describe a forgetful rabbit?**

A hare-brain.

8. **Where did the Easter Bunny go for his morning breakfast?**

IHOP.

9. **How does a bunny normally travel?**

By a hare plane.

10. **Are carrots good for your vision?**

Have you ever seen the Easter Bunny wear glasses?

11.   Where does the Easter Bunny find all of his Easter eggs?

At an eggplant.

12.   What do you call an annoying rabbit?

Bugs Bunny.

13.   What do you call a bunny that has fleas?

Bugs Bunny!

14.   What type of bean grows in the Easter Bunny's garden?

Jelly beans.

15.   What made the father Easter egg crack?

The mother Easter egg told him a funny joke.

16.   What comes from honey and a rabbit?

A honey bunny.

17.   How does the Easter Bunny comb it's hair?

With a hare brush.

18.   How does the Easter Bunny dry it's hair?

With a hare dryer!

19. **How does keep it's hair so neat and shiny?**

With hare spray!

20. **What happens when you mix an elephant and a rabbit?**

An elephant that always eats his carrots.

21.   What did one Easter egg say to the other?

Heard any good yolks lately?

22.   What kind of music does the Easter bunny listen to?

Hip Hop.

23.   What did the clever rabbit say to the carrot?

It has been so nice gnawing you.

24.   Why did the Easter chick hide?

He was just a little chicken.

25. **What gives away the location of the Easter bunny?**

Eggs mark the spot.

26. **How do you send a letter to the Easter bunny?**

Hare mail.

27. **What made the egg crack?**

He was tickled.

28. **What do you call a rabbit with a cold?**

Runny bunny.

29.   Why did the bunny have to hop down the trail?

He wasn't old enough to drive.

30.   What did the Easter bunny say after his trip?

It was egg-cellent.

31.   What happens when a rabbit throws a tantrum?

He gets hopping angry.

32.   Who paints all of the Easter bunny's eggs?

Santa's elves when they are in off-season.

33.   What kind of dance does the Easter bunny do?

The bunny hop.

34.   What kinds of stories does the Easter bunny like?

Stories that feature hoppy endings.

35. Why is a bunny so lucky?

Because it has four rabbits feet.

36. What made the Easter bunny cross the road?

Because the Easter Chic's stole his eggs.

37. How does Easter always end?

With the letter R.

38. What come from an insect and a rabbit being crossed?

Bugs Bunny

39. **Why was the girl rabbit so upset?**

She was having a bad hare day.

40. **Why don't you pour hot water down a rabbit hole?**

Because you get a hot cross bunny.

41. **What do you call a genius bunny?**

An egg head.

42. **How does the Easter bunny leave a bulding?**

The emergency egg-set.

43.   What do bunnies do to stay in shape?

Egg-ercise.

44.   What day of the week does an Easter egg fear?

Fry-day.

45. **Why do people paint Easter eggs?**

It is quite difficult to wallpaper them.

46. **What do you call someone who is addicted to eggs?**

An egg-oholic.

47.   What did the Easter bunny say to get more cheese on his omelet?

I want egg-stra cheese.

48.   What do you call an awesome Easter egg?

Egg-ceptional.

49. **What do you call a perfect number of eggs?**

The egg-act amount.

50. **What did the Easter bunny say when they went on he went on the rollercoaster?**

This is egg-citing!

51.   How did the Easter bunny feel when they found all of their eggs?

Egg-static.

52.   What kind of dance does the Easter bunny like to attend?

An egg-stravagant one.

53. **How does the Easter Bunny hop so high?**

Egg-splosive jumps.

54. **What do you call a daredevil Easter egg?**

Egg-stream.

55. **What kind of egg expands the truth?**

One who likes to egg-zaggerate.

56. **Where did the Easter bunny go to lunch?**

Chicken Egg-spress.

57.   How do you capture the Easter bunny?

Hide in a garden and make noises like a carrot.

58.   What do you call a dumb bunny?

A hare brain.

59.   How do you catch a unique bunny?

You 'nique up on him.

60.   How many hairs will you find in a bunny's tail?

Zero. They are on the outside.

61. **What would you call a line of rabbits that are walking backwards?**

A receding hare-line.

62. **How are rabbits most like a calculator?**

They can multiply very fast.

63. **Why is a rabbit's nose never 12 inches long?**

Then it would be a foot silly.

64. **How can you tell that a rabbit is old?**

It has grey hares.

65.   How do you know you are eating rabbit stew?

It contains hare.

66.   What kind of rabbit tells the best jokes?

A funny bunny.

67. What would you call a rabbit that lives in Antarctica?

Very cold.

68. What is something that only rabbits have?

Baby rabbits.

69. What would you call a bunny with an encyclopedia in his pocket?

A smarty pants.

70. What comes from a spider and the Easter Bunny?

A harenet.

71. What does the Easter bunny do to stay fit?

Hare-batics.

72. What is the difference between a fake bill and a crazy rabbit?

One is a mad bunny, and the other is fake money.

73.   Why did the Easter egg hide from the children?

He was a little chicken.

74.   How many Easter eggs can you fit into an empty basket?

One. Afterwards, it is no longer empty.

75. **What has long ears, grows in trees, and is yellow?**

The Easter banana.

76. **What did the Easter bunny say about his dinner?**

It was egg-cellent.

77.   What is the favorite state capital of the Easter bunny?

Albunny, New York.

78.   Where does a vampire keep his Easter eggs?

In his Easter cofin.

79.   Who did the Easter bunny call to rid his house of bugs?

The egg-sterminator.

80.   Where does the Easter bunny get all of his eggs from?

The egg-plant.

81.   What would you call the Easter bunny the day after Easter?

Very tired.

82.   What do you call a Easter bunny on Mars?

an Egg-straterrestrial.

83.   Why was the duck fired by the Easter bunny?

He kept quacking the eggs.

84.   What is wrong with all of these Easter jokes?

They crack you up.

85. Why did the Easter bunny leave school?

He was egg-spelled.

86. What is an Easter eggs best sport?

Running.

87.   Why did the Easter bunny have a shiny nose?

The powder puff was on the other end.

88.   Why did the bunny want to go to the ball?

They wanted to do the bunny hop.

89. Why did the Easter bunny cross the road?

It wanted to prove it wasn't a chicken.

90. What did the Easter bunny name his son?

Hare-ry.

91.   What is the Easter bunny's favorite sport?

Basket-ball.

92. What is the main difference between a lumberjack and a rabbit?

Once chews and hops, the other saws and chops.

93. What did the confused rabbit say?

I have no I d-ear.

94. What is the Easter bunny's favorite game?

Pin the tail on the rabbit

95. Why are Easter eggs scared to go out at night?

Incase they have a cracking time.

96. How does the Easter chick party?

Around the cluck.

97. What is the Easter bunny's favorite classic story?

A cotton tale.

98. How did the Easter bunny leave the highway?

It took the egg-sit.

99. What did the tired Easter egg say?

I'm egg-sausted.

100. Why do you stuff Easter candy into your mouth?

It isn't as good stuffed in your ears.

101. What did the Easter egg do when the light turned green?

It egg-celerated.

102. Who is the best actor, according to the Easter bunny?

Rabbit De Niro.

103. What happens when you cross a stressed man with the Easter bunny?

You get a basket case.

104. Why did the Easter bunny miss his flight?

He didn't have hare fare.

35547555R00031

Made in the USA
Lexington, KY
04 April 2019